ALTAR

Desree is an award-winning writer, spoken word artist, educator and producer based in London and Slough. An alumna of Born::Free Writers' Collective, Jerwood Arts Poetry In Performance Programme and the Obsidian Foundation, Desree was Poet in Residence at Glastonbury Festival 2022 and for Slough's EMPOWORD. A familiar voice on BBC Radio Berkshire, her work has been broadcast on Sky Arts' *The Life and Rhymes of Benjamin Zephaniah*; and published in *JOY//US Poems of Queer Joy*, *Ink Sweat & Tears*, Spoken Word London's *Anti-Hate Anthology* and more. She performs across the UK and internationally. Her sell-out self-published pamphlet, *I Find My Strength in Simple Things* (2017) was published in second edition by Burning Eye Books in 2021. *Altar* is her first collection.

BY THE SAME AUTHOR

I Find My Strength in Simple Things
(2017. Second edition Burning Eye Books, 2021)

Altar

DESREE

BAD BETTY PRESS

First published in 2025 by Bad Betty Press
Cobden Place, Cobden Chambers, Nottingham NG1 2ED

badbettypress.com

PB ISBN: 978-1-913268-72-5
EPUB ISBN: 978-1-913268-73-2

A CIP record of this book is available from the British Library.

Book design by Amy Acre

Printed and bound in the UK by TJ Books Limited, Padstow, Cornwall using FSC® Certified paper from responsibly managed forests

MIX
Paper | Supporting responsible forestry
FSC
www.fsc.org
FSC® C013056

LOTTERY FUNDED
ARTS COUNCIL ENGLAND
Supported using public funding by
ARTS COUNCIL ENGLAND

For Eunice Carty,
an arsenal of magic and redemption.
I am never not thinking of you.

For my wife,
who taught me that to be brave is to be vulnerable.

CONTENTS

The Notorious B.I.G. and Jesus Christ on a Boat 11
Salvo 12
Flat 14
Goose 15
E.g., 16
Stop dat 18
A Woman From Work Moves to Peckham and Tries to Find Damilola Taylor's Resting Place or Six Facts About Fungi 19
Eight 21
Empty 22
Sign of the Cross 23
On Going to Anguilla to Bury My Grandad 24
We Bury Our Own 25
Start dat 27
You Know a Jumbee by the Taste of Their Umbrella 28
Intruders 29
Sonnet for Eunice 31
do/do not 32
Get dat 34
Sitient 35
Guide Me O Thou Great Redeemer, 36
Parallel 42
What? 43
Oddjob 44
Kim K Takes a Photo of Sarah Baartman to Her Surgeon 45

Rum 46
Hail 47
cockroaches 48
Disclosure 49
Before i knew love, 51
gold 52
Liraglutide 53
the break-up 54
It's 1.26am, I'm queuing for a bagel in Stoke Newington and Chris Brown jumps the line 55
tell yourself, 56
Cheese 58
Burst 59
Copy 60
for safekeeping 62
Crown 63
Call It Halo 65
Today, 66

Notes 68
Acknowledgements 70

Altar

THE NOTORIOUS B.I.G. AND JESUS CHRIST ON A BOAT

Then, without warning, a furious storm came. Billows big enough to separate the weak from the obsolete. Biggie sucks saliva from behind his teeth, throws his hands in da air and Jesus sighs. Waves permeate the cleats of the boat, like bullets, and drive by.

Sweat dances down Biggie's cheek. Finally, Jesus asks *Why are you so afraid?* Biggie pats his wallet to check his pride is still there; he wants forgiveness, but Jesus too has cast out all that sold and bought on his block.

There is no greater love than this—that a man should lay down his life for his friends. Biggie shifts from the stern to the gunwale. The boat does not falter. Jesus takes out a crustless tuna sandwich, pulls it apart from the middle, hands half to Biggie. They chew watching the waves turn to foam as the sky hums a perfect blue.

SALVO

after Hala Alyan

darling slough,
i love you like rain.

when the boy put a brick to aaron's head,
blood littered the feet of our estate.
red next to yesterday's water bombs.

no one called this a war. the only shrapnel
on these streets: needles, laces
that held veins tighter than purse strings.

there was no clearly uniformed opp—
only ideas, small as a mentos dropped
into coke before exploding on pavement
outside his little brother's bedroom.

darling slough,
i love you like rain.

graveyard with no tombstones.
adventure playground some children
play on, others lie underneath.

i can't walk through the newbuilds
without hearing the men i loved
bleating inside you.

darling slough,
i love you like rain.

i have mistaken the wind, echoing
through the vacant aisles, for applause,
bowed to the shop fronts, a reflection
of acclaim attempting to double its value.

darling slough,
i love you like rain.

forgive me for telling on you.
i saw a bear in the field during rounders.
or was it a panther? maybe

it was the soldiers outside tesco
ready to feast. i watch them devour a boy
and spit out the bones of a bird.

every predator is prey to what swallows them.

Flat like home.
Grenfell, like Tottenham.
Like New Cross, like
Rise like fire.
High like almost.
from touching them.
the stars but prohibited
on. High enough to see
they carried her body out
dreams. Like the stretcher
to get to. Flat like
Nothing safe will be easy
life will be a climb.
Stairs because
What a long-standing joke.
staircase. Nothing rises.
like Sidney lying in the
Troublesome. High
a seagull. Far from flat.
you from. Tall enough to punch
Higher than God could catch

FLAT

GOOSE

Forty-three percent of Premier League
football players are Black. Kin with
the flattened earth embedded
between studs. Even when
they're the ones shooting
they are always
considered
target.
Duck.

E.G.,

Block (noun) a large, solid piece of hard material, especially rock, stone or wood, typically with flat surfaces on each side

e.g., Dale got a key in the shape of a block.

Key (adjective) of crucial importance

e.g., The wraps in the car were a key piece of evidence to ensure Dale grew up without his big brother.

Wrap (verb) to cover or enclose in paper or soft material

e.g., Dale's mum wrapped her arms around his brother, Jake, when the judge gave him a bird.

Bird (noun) a warm blooded vertebrate that is covered with feathers and has two wings and two legs

e.g., Now that Jake's line was free, Dale had seen more cats fly than birds.

Line (noun) a row or series

e.g., Brown lining his waistband, Dale's bike

arrived and cats queued around the block like Swifties.

Brown (adjective) a dark tertiary colour with a yellowish or reddish hue

e.g., After getting nicked, Dale saw leaves turn brown to green three times.

Nicked (verb) to cut into or wound slightly

e.g., Outside on his seventeenth birthday, he nicked himself shaving away adulthood before going to link his boys.

Link (noun) a connecting element or factor

e.g., They were able to link Dale to the murder from the fingerprints left on the shank.

Shank (noun) a straight, narrow section between the two ends of a tool or object

e.g., He counted backwards every time the key's shank thundered in its lock: 5,476.

Stop dat

The last days I was my brother's
eldest sibling I was told by a child
that my voice sounded like
I had a rose stuck in my throat

A WOMAN FROM WORK MOVES TO PECKHAM AND TRIES TO FIND DAMILOLA TAYLOR'S RESTING PLACE OR SIX FACTS ABOUT FUNGI

1. While spores can be dormant for extended periods, given advantageous conditions, they continue to grow. Once spores break dormancy, fungi become active, growing and reproducing, stifling whole communities.

2. When fungal spores germinate, germlings absorb all the nutrients around them. The cytoplasm becomes active and nuclear division occurs.

3. Although less than 5% of fungi are poisonous, those that are resemble their edible counterparts, making them especially dangerous. Symptoms may not occur immediately but, once triggered, prove deadly.

4. Parasitic fungi feed off their host. Evolving to feast off different matter, many have a special organ called a haustoria which allows them to tear deeper into the host's living tissue.

5. Invasive species can infest a new area by accident or intentionally. To establish themselves, they must reproduce quickly, adapt with ease, and suppress the indigenous flora and fauna, property or economy.

6. Fungi are classified as being in a kingdom of their own. Within this kingdom: the largest organism on the planet. It spans land it finds habitable and kills what's already there.

EIGHT

Family portrait, taken on a pink
Fujifilm Finepix, breathes
on the mantel at Nan's house.

Mouths reticent with ache
distort for the flash.

Screaming looks a lot
like laughing when taken
from the right angle.

EMPTY

Stolen half-pint glasses and hand-me-down
cutlery sit among dust, behind markless
drawer handles. Silence fights against fridge's
muffled screams.

Lights ward off material thieves. Memories find
home in bereft cupboards and behind
photographs. Security cameras long to light up
more than abandoned leaves.

Imprints have pushed their way out of sofas and
gather quieted. Settle between unsullied
figurines and good china. Stoic, Alexa waits
to be asked for the time by the woman
always humming *old rugged cross.*

Inside the stillness, pain and growth are bickering
like siblings. Lights go up,

SIGN OF THE CROSS

Like everyone else, I bow my head,
as though fishing somewhere shallow
enough to see my reflection amongst
the stones. I meet the sea of people
dressed heavy and dark like the marlin
I have caught, which sits moonless and
heavy on my chest.

I look down at my feet knowing
I'm too short to hold all this longing.
That the blood of this catch will impel
gaping eyes with arms too weak to reel.

I do not pick up my feet to reach the
altar. Instead, harpoon my own prayer.
Whiskey, straight. Water. Raise my glass,
plastic, plucked from the shelf inside
the liquor store next to the funeral
parlour. Hold the line with both hands.

Amen.

ON GOING TO ANGUILLA TO BURY MY GRANDAD

watching the sunrise
on shoal bay
isn't that the most poem
you've ever heard
two rising bodies
of saltwater returning

WE BURY OUR OWN

black suits
black ties
white shirts
black skin
brown mud
on black
dress shoes
we bury
our own

clear rain
grey skies
white tissues
filled with
grief brown
mud hits
new resting
place brown
mud brown
mud brown
mud black
dress shoes
we bury
our own

black suit
jackets cradled
by loved
ones spades
shovels
forks held
by hands
still trying
to hold
onto brown
mud black
dress shoes
we bury
our own

Start dat

I had a rose stuck in my throat
I made gun fingers out of bruised
hands, screaming *don't stop,*
don't stop, 'til it's hurting

YOU KNOW A JUMBEE BY THE TASTE OF THEIR UMBRELLA

or the felled moss-covered wood
commemorating a life lived   or lost
          in a single epitaph.   By their crinkling
fog, or the crispness of their shadow.

Reluctantly, the rain makes space
          for death.   When sliced
flesh grows   out of
          phantom limbs,

          greying winds lash
against weathered stone.
          When great trees fall,
fruit grows   within them.

INTRUDERS

1992, I arrived with a body too small to carry anything but concrete and chimneys. I returned each year and, like they had taught me in school, called it mine.

Anguilla was first home to Indigenous Amerindian peoples who put home on their back and roved from South America.

I buried my tongue under the accent hoping to abstract the coral and limestone. I built sandcastles by an ocean clear enough to see the red, white and blue anchors. Telling stories of Motherland to the children she had tried to drown.

Some claim Columbus was the first marauder of these sands, whiter than the hands of its thieves.

Oh, small island people. Do you not hear the settler in this accent? How I have come here to take what does not belong to me, name it ancestry. All I know of this land is what my grandmother taught me, we courtesy to the same Queen.

Others claim it was René Goulaine de Laudonnière…

Oh, small island people, with hair straight as rulers, they consumed everything, took what wasn't offered, planted tobacco and sugar in your bloodline and claimed ignorance when the cancer spread.

Malliouhana, Arrow-head, they took your name,
then baptised you Eel: slippery, mysterious, needing
to be caught.

SONNET FOR EUNICE

Her mother, Adina, sculpted her from clay
on an island small enough to fold in half.
God Herself delivered superhuman gifts:
courage to sail sixteen ships, to raise
flour and yeast into Zion before the sun
took its first breath. Hands that ordered
stems into oasis, hope into prayer.
A mouth that held secrets only as long
as it took to boil rice, but held joy close
enough to taste. Look at her! An arsenal
of magic and redemption. A song in retreat.
Scripture baptised in wrinkles. Giver of ceremony.
        Eunice, sanctuary lives between your fingers.
        Grandmother, at your feet I find my sacrarium.

DO/DO NOT

make eye contact
look for fathers in dead things
watch my wife and kids
get wrathful
complain about masculinity
keep mini-milks in your back pocket
marry the woman you love
walk yourself down the aisle
invite him only to the evening
miss him
look for fathers in dead things
remember winning and peace aren't synonyms
listen to the temptations or
madonna or
buck owens
stretch after exercise
take seamoss or
aloe vera gel or
whatever pyramid scheme your cousin's pushing
keep a clean house
tell everyone that it doesn't hurt
look for fathers in dead things
buy a cat
turn off the desmonds and
moonlight and
black-ish
read bell hooks

read ta-nehisi coates
read
look for fathers from the sky
forget uncle phil or
your grandad
dream
be your own father
become a thing of no use
look for similarities between the two
turn off the desmonds
burn the remote
displace him from your veins
close your borders
wish him into where you are
wish yourself into where he is
drinking kestrels playing
dominoes laughing so loud
he can't hear his children
          screaming

Get dat

I screamed *don't stop,*
don't stop 'til it's bleeding
as I tried to pull out the rose
before it bloomed

SITIENT

i would not still
be begging to taste his voice if
i knew the difference between love
and sacrifice i would have learned how
to pray for my own happiness
would have stopped praying
only for yours

if i had known the number of casualties
caused by empty mouths and closed fists
i would have made cups out of
these hands, held them under
your eyes
so that you could drink yourself
full.

GUIDE ME O THOU GREAT REDEEMER,

For the lips of a harlot are like a honeycomb dropping, and her throat is smoother than oil.
Proverbs 5:3

STAND My class walks hand in hand to the Catholic church that sits behind my primary school playground. The back of my skirt is riding up the part of my body that I grow to hate, and love, and let define me. I know Matthew can feel my panic melt to sweat between our palms. With ten of my fingers clasped, afraid to move in case they realise the porosity of this flesh, all I can think about is what my Nan would say if I *sho mi ass in chuch.* I don't know if it is here I learn that the only way to have a body is to pretend you don't. To tug and pull at it and wish to be water. I look at the Virgin Mary and understand. To be a good girl is to know that this body isn't mine and must only be used in service.

SIT Inside Cologne Cathedral, our eyes lock. With his arms outstretched, he wears nothing but a cloth and a pout, a hushed sigh hanging loosely from his brow. I look around and see that same brow on every face, on every wall, in every corner. Eyes blue enough to part the red sea or birth a son of god his countrymen wouldn't recognise. I light a candle for a friend. Instinctively I bow my head in the only way I've been taught to still grief; our father, our father, our father. I pray this is the last time I must ask a white man for anything.

STAND Colene's dad takes unripe bananas to Arsenal games. As I walk the playground I can smell last night's game in the seams of shirts. And the match begins. Sides picked, the air is dry. Someone renames me *Toby* as they pass me a hospital ball. Forced into defence, I put in a shift and run it off. In this playground I will learn how to be a box-to-box player, how to hug the line.

SIT A boy with hair
like wool and feet
of burnt bronze tells me girls
with skin deeper than soil
just aren't that attractive. I ask
about the calluses on his mum's
hands, what anchors his roots
and what he will use to grow
his garden if not earth and clay
and mud? Our eyes lock. With
arms outstretched, a hushed
sigh hanging loosely from his
brow, he remembers the best
way to till soil is with your fists.

KNEEL I arrive to church on Jesus' birthday wearing last night's mistakes and a faux fur jacket, attempting to squeeze myself into the pews. My breath still hot from consecrating all that wine. My head bowed, shame dresses as silence; holy bodies must be broken and consumed. I place one hand on top of the other to receive the body of Christ. I wonder if this where I learned what consent looks like. On my knees, with my palms up.

PARALLEL

Somewhere, I didn't cut my eyebrow on the step, my face
never dripped crimson. There is a version of me without scars.
One where my mum doesn't take the ring, or doesn't take it off.
My dad decides not to give it to her, never swallows it whole.
Let's say I stop after three Skittle vodka shots at Turtle bar.
Or four. No one borrows my legs, or my mouth, or my cunt.
Nan tore her dress running to catch her dreams' condensation
and SS Ipeno left without her. I never go to that reading,
on that day, in that venue. He never tattoos his name
around my ankle like a bracelet. Or perhaps, I don't know,
maybe all those versions of me exist inside of this one
and I must melt myself down, sluice for them.

What?

Before it bloomed, the rose
had made space between
my teeth and rested its
edges on my tongue

ODDJOB

Here, in this office, I am Oddjob.
Squat arms like thighs, a sickly zoo-smell.
I do not have a razor-edged hat, or the ability to
choose when strangers touch my hair. My words
sit eagerly in the sink, next to the coffee machine.
With every pregnant pause my pupils dilate just
enough to let the silence crown without tearing.
Each time my voice feels ready for this new birth
it proves to be another false labour. Sarah reminds
me that the words of Black women have a much
longer gestation period. I can't work out if I'm a
mute or if I've been turned off at the wall.
Maybe this is just another forced sterilisation.

KIM K TAKES A PHOTO OF SARAH BAARTMAN TO HER SURGEON

The surgeon nods,
scarifies a note
or two, captures
a photo. Studies
Sarah's ass, looks
for a scar left from
an incision. Kim coughs. Sighs.
Asks if he can do what God did
not. Pilfer the 'hot' from Hottentot.
Give her that slim, thique, steatopygic
silhouette. 'I want to be the number
one freak at this show. I want people
to wonder about my origins. Get
me a tight fitted garment, a
crowd and I will give
you just enough, so it
looks like consent'.

RUM

Sometimes, white rum is filtered
to distil colours that would taint
its white tint. Once rid of its
congeners, it is often described as
refined.

Dark rum is aged in charred barrels reacting
to the characteristics of its environment.
As a result, it is strong and usually shot.

HAIL

Kano gig   on the dimly lit
uneven floor   of Brixton Academy
a man lowers himself   with the grace
of falling plates   the front
of his crotch   directly level
with the magnetic strip of my ass
all in time   to 126 bpm
I feel the air   his open shirt has created
my own   personal   wind machine
am I supposed to feel   grateful
it's funny   do you remember
in The Office   when Jim bought Pam
a house   without telling her   or
That '70s Show   when Eric
broke up with Donna   because
she wouldn't   wear his promise ring
or   when Ross   told Rachel
they were getting married
I'm in high waisted jeans
a t-shirt   politely tucked in
I can feel his knees   against my
hamstring   step out of his way
step out of my way   he steps
forward   I step out of his way
step out of my way   he steps forward
I look at him   stealing my living
with his sticky fingers   Kano raps
no I don't know the Queen   but
that bitch stays in my jean pocket

COCKROACHES

for the men who scream at me on my run

In this movie, a man slams
his fist and screams before
landing on a cockroach.

Luckily cockroaches
don't have ears
therefore cannot hear
the sound, reminding
them their body
is disposable.

DISCLOSURE

i

he fucked me in the park
i didn't want to

did she say *r*pe* though?
we have to be careful
with our language

boys like him always get
away with these things

what does she expect
the school to do?
are you sure?

they moved him and expected
everything to be fine

you have to understand
she is quite difficult
to talk to

ii

Dark skinned girls are born with aphonia.
There are several preventative measures:
skin lightening cream, empathy, ingesting
bleach, martial arts training.
One has proven to be effective.

BEFORE I KNEW LOVE,

i knew secrets. i learnt
them like roots learn
soil

i knew bodies built
in the image of a fireplace
were only useful if there
was something burning
inside them. i learnt
safety means between
flames

i knew i was a figment
of some guy's reverie
Catholic schoolboys with
ties striped like a tiger will
teach you how to want more
but graciously accept
less

GOLD

there is enough gold inside the earth to coat the planet so
on wednesday i bought myself a necklace my bank
balance pinched my abdomen so i bought myself a foot
spa if that is not self-care, then i don't know what is
my therapist loves a joke and thinks i'm hilarious so i told her
about my depression and how sometimes i [redacted]
i bought myself a new dress because who can be sad in a
new dress i can quite easily apparently

LIRAGLUTIDE

I'm telling my doctor about a cough
I've had for 3 months. He advises me
on ways I can make myself smaller.
I'm coughing. He asks if I've considered
exercise. *His stethoscope creaks.*
I show him the lump under my armpit.
He presses his fingers around my wings
and clips them. He asks me if I have
been tested for diabetes.
He offers me Saxenda.

My body is wrong—
the doctor thinks it needs a shot.

THE BREAK-UP

In a few minutes, we said more to each other than we had
in two years.

'Thank you' ricocheted off our pathetic beating
hearts and landed somewhere between forever and
goodbye.

We sat opposite one another and watched the space we finally
gave rock our egos to a peaceful rest.

Speaker turned into microphone now the cries had stopped.

We walked, like we had done before, except further apart and
smiling, like two people who had loved once, and
enough, to leave each other the hell alone.

IT'S 1.26AM, I'M QUEUING FOR A BAGEL IN STOKE NEWINGTON AND CHRIS BROWN JUMPS THE LINE

I wonder if this is the handshake for violence and I missed it. Have always missed it. Did you know once a male angler fish sinks his teeth into the female, mating has begun? Did you know that Chris Brown took Karrueche to a diner on their first date? He mutters something about an apology, and I clench my right fist. Once a man I loved reminded me about the pillowy nature of both conviction and flesh. Just as the woman behind me pulls out her phone, a single tear drops from his left eye. And I think of Issac Newton inventing the cat flap, but cat flaps having already existed. I duck.

TELL YOURSELF,

as you rest your curving spine against the straight
dining room chair, as your family call her
your *friend* over the macaroni cheese,
that they have always loved you

tell yourself,
the lips you purse to extinguish the heat
of your grandma's hot chocolate is the same
lips with which you kiss your girlfriend

tell yourself,
when your best friend sings towards
what she might call heaven 'batty man fi dead',
that it is only a song, that it is only many songs,
sing along

tell yourself,
as your uncle flings 'faggot' at the television
while you write your gay little poems in the kitchen,
that he is from a different time, a different place

tell yourself,
you and your girlfriend's bed is an altar
that does not require sacrifice

tell yourself
as you weave your bodies between one another
that you are not a tapestry,
and you do not have to hang to prove you exist.

CHEESE

Whilst travelling, I often joked
I wasn't pretty enough to be kidnapped.

As the twentieth local asked for my photo,
I realised how rare it was for people
to see black women, happy, free.

Happy Black Women are endangered
and must be shot at every opportunity.

BURST

The average heartbeat of a woman is
eight beats a minute faster than a man's
and I feel that in the way she loves me.
Her hands cradle all my joy, even though
we've both seen the impact of tremors.
Her eyes find the truths I hid between the
bricks in my mother's house. Once, at the
beginning she loved me too hard, and
the clay started to come away from the
wall. So we built scaffolding out of plane
tickets and pray for only the smallest of storms.

COPY

the first time we said I love you
we had lined the
inside of our mouths
with spirits
had just ran out of hope,
but were handed our breath back.
we two
spooned on a single bed
entangled.
I love you
burnt the back of our throats
like a spliff with too much tobacco
we saw gold
between broken pieces.
we watched a boxing match
in my childhood living room
my parents
a thermocline,
a pocket of heat, but
you held
everything
I had to give,

I had to give
everything.
you held
a pocket of heat,
a thermocline
my parents
in my childhood living room;
we watched a boxing match
between broken pieces.
they saw gold
like a spliff with too much tobacco
burn the back of their throat.
I love you
entangled,
spooning on a single bed.
The two
had just ran out of hope
with spirits
inside of their mouths
they had lied
the first time they said I love you

FOR SAFEKEEPING

start slow subtle i want to be felt
barely touched
not touched at all i want purposeful
long
involved decisive
tell me with that mouth
what your fingers will find next
the soft brush of your lip against my pubic bone
tell me who you are where do you want
these hands i have searched your warmness
found it under thighs in the space between
hands between
eyes be gentle sure with my eyes closed
i want to reach far enough
inside to find the pieces of me i gave to you
for safekeeping

CROWN

she could have
had horns, i'd have still
praised her godliness.

because god made light,
i see that between her fingers.
how her hands stitch and fluff
and shape what was formless.

each curl embracing the other
only separated by wide teeth or
hands patient enough to turn
shea into stardust.

because god made skies,
and every part of her points
to it. and i wonder if i have
believed her into existence.

she is looking at me, looking at her.

i catch myself, *cough,*
say what all black women
say to each other in the bathroom;

I love your hair sis.

CALL IT HALO

They say nothing and everything to not call it halo.
Circle of bright, white light, they won't call it halo.

They say strong as though it is the same as beautiful.
You wear hardship on your head and call it halo.

History pressed pinks and purples in the red of your blood.
You bandaged your wounds up, and called it halo.

Sis, they are intimidated by you, you are
not intimidating, and still they cannot call it halo.

The world in your womb yet they attack you.
Castor oil in your joy, call it halo.

Everything made in your image. The nebulae created
this pigment. Radiating light until they call it halo.

Natural, weave, curls loose or tight. Hijab,
head wrap worn with pride, now they call it halo.

I love you. I am learning how to love me,
praise you like a deity, and always call it halo.

TODAY,

i do not want to jump off anything
a building is just a building

my eulogy is not etched into the climbing frame at the
back of
my primary school playground or engraved in the
window at VFD.

i cut into my fish and stop when i hit the bone.
today the sun is out, and i look my best for her.

NOTES

The poems 'Stop dat' (p18), 'Start dat' (p27), 'Get dat' (p34) and 'What?' (p43) are inspired by Dizzee Rascal's track 'Stop Dat' from his album *Boy in da Corner,* XL Recordings, 2003.

'Sign of the Cross' (p23) draws on the imagery and language of *The Old Man and the Sea* by Ernest Hemingway, Charles Scribner's Sons, 1952.

In 'You Know a Jumbee by the Taste of Their Umbrella' (p28), a Jumbee is a type of mythological spirit or demon in the folklore of some Caribbean countries, Jumbee umbrella is an alternative name for a mushroom in some Caribbean countries, and the words 'When great trees fall' are taken from 'When Great Trees Fall' by Maya Angelou (*I Shall Not Be Moved*, 1990, Random House).

'Intruders' (p29) incorporates historical references sourced from the Government of Anguilla Archives' *Anguilla History*.

In 'Oddjob' (p44), the descriptions 'squat', 'arms like thighs' and a 'sickly zoo-smell' are taken from descriptions of the character Oddjob in the James Bond films and novels.

'Parallel' (p42) includes a ship called the *SS Ipeno*. My grandmother told me this is the ship that she came to the UK on, however I have never been able to find any records of it. Still, she knew everything so...

ACKNOWLEDGEMENTS

Maddy, my first (and on publication of this book, only) wife. You make the world sing the most perfect song and have taught me the lyrics. Forever hardly feels like enough time.

Nan, Grandad, Nanny Maule and Grandaddy Mac – my favourite poets and storytellers. Thank you for all you did so I can write silly little poems.

Mum, Dad, Shak, Kenisha – till the motherf' wheels fall off and still even when the rims are scraping the ground.

Becci, Ben, Jamie, Ty – thank you for always feeling like family.

Kairo, Azari, Elijah, Kyze, Sienna, Kade – my babies. There is no version of me that will not be holding your hand or your heart, forever.

Bianca, Karimah, Safiya, your strength is in how deeply you love, and I am so grateful to have sisters that I can meditate with but also aren't afraid to grab Vaseline and a bally.

Annabelle, Tanya, Emma – thank you for always holding my hand as you push me off the cliff.

You are joy and the best type of family.

Hannah Gordon, how lucky am I to have someone who grows me as a poet and a person. Thank you for sharing your knowledge and your joy with me.

Bad Betty team, thank you for believing in my work and in me. Amy, to be held by you through this editing process has been so joyful. Thank you for taking your time with me.

Rachel Long, learning and sharing with you, once a month in 2021 completely changed the way I think about writing and the type of facilitator I am – I am grateful to and for you.

I am immensely grateful to all the spaces where these poems were born, nurtured, and shaped. Thank you to Arts Council England Project funding, Malika's Poetry Kitchen, Obsidian Retreat, Words First (BBC Radio 1Xtra), Poetry School, malakaï sargeant, Belinda Zhawi and Born::Free Writers' Collective, Rob and the Together As One team, Harry, George and the Word Of Mouth LDN team, Jerwood Arts Poetry in Performance, Anthony Anaxagorou and Apples & Snakes. Thank you for providing the workshops, communities, and inspiration that have been instrumental in the creation of this collection.

Aditi Banerjee, Caleb Femi, Courtney Conrad, Dauda Ladejobi, Eljae, Joelle Taylor, Kareem Parkins-Brown, Kat Holmes, Lakesha Arie-Angelou, lisa luxx, Repeat Beat Poet, Safaa Bensom-Effiom, Simone Carty, Tasneim Zyaad, Usaama Minhas, Yomi Ṣode and all the incredible artists I have come into contact with over the years: your work, and your commitment to it, is a constant reminder of hope and freedom and resistance, and how we will one day have them all.

Thank you to some of these poems' first homes: *Finished Creatures*, *Icarus*, *Fly on the Wall Magazine*, *Wetgrain*, *Joy//Us*. I am deeply grateful for your belief in my work.

Free Congo, Free Palestine, Free Sudan, Free Haiti.

Freedom is never given; it is won – A. Philip Randolph